WHAT'S NEXT?

By Pastor Terence E. Lee

D1343105

Dorrance Publishing Co
585 Alpha Drive
Pittsburgh, PA 15238
Visit our website at www.dorrancebookstore.com

ISBN: 979-8-88729-164-2
eISBN: 979-8-88729-664-7

TABLE OF CONTENTS

INTRODUCTION

People have been wondering for hundreds of years what tomorrow holds. Some people are frantic with fear, and some think they have it all figured out. Where do we look for the answers to our questions? Certainly not to the feeble wisdom of men. In truth there is only one place that we can go to find out what tomorrow holds: the Bible, the Word of God. The Bible is infallible and inerrant. It provides us with all the answers we need concerning the future. But in order to know, we must study the Bible. There is no other book in the world like that book. 2 Timothy 2:15 tells us, "Study to show thyself approved unto God, a workman that needeth not to be ashamed, rightly dividing the word of truth." Psalm 119:105 states, "Thy word is a lamp unto my feet and a light unto my path." It is in God's word that we find out what is next, and what we are to do. If we follow God's instructions we will never fail. He will walk with us through the good times and the bad. He promises that He will never leave us or forsake us. Because we do not understand everything, we must live every day of our lives by faith.

Hebrews 11:6 states, "Without faith, it is impossible to please God, for he that cometh to God must believe that he is and a Rewarder of them that diligently seek Him." Everything is hinged on faith beginning with our eternal salvation, Ephesians 2:8–9 states, "For by grace are ye saved, through faith, and that not of yourselves, it is the gift of God, not of works lest any man should boast." Faith is very simply taking God at His word. Believing that He will do what He says He will do. It is impossible for God to lie because every word that proceeds out of His mouth is truth. God promises that if we trust in His gospel, He will save us from an eternity in hell. Salvation is the first step of faith that gives the proper understanding of His word. The moment we are saved, we receive the gift of His Holy Spirit to help us understand His word. We cannot know what is next until we are redeemed by the blood of the Lamb. God wants to share with His people His plans for the ages. Throughout the Bible, time has been measured by certain people and events.

Examples:
1-Man's fall and the promise of a coming Savior
2-The great flood
3-Abraham's call
4-The birth of Jacob
5-Egyptian bondage and the exodus from Egypt
6-The giving of the law
7-The ascension of David to the throne of Israel
8-The age of the prophets
9-John the Baptist appears
10-Jesus, God's Lamb appears
11-The death, burial, and resurrection of Jesus
12-Jesus's ascension and promise of His return

It is at this point we will begin our study on "WHAT'S NEXT?" We must ask of ourselves where are we now according to God's biblical calendar? According to Scripture, we are now in a period of waiting. We are waiting on the promise of God to be fulfilled, which is the first part of the second coming of Jesus. The second coming will be divided into two parts. The Rapture of the Saints and the actual return of Jesus to the earth."

CHAPTER I
THE RAPTURE OF THE SAINTS

All through the New Testament we are told that Jesus is coming again. God has a plan for the ages, and He wants His people to know what it is. He is always up front, never trying to hide anything from His people. Therefore, it is a great joy to study His plan as we continue to move through the ages. The next great event to take place is the first part of the second coming, "The Rapture of the Saints." In John 14:1–3 Jesus said, "I go to prepare a place for you. And if I go and prepare a place for you, I will come again and receive you unto Myself that where I am there ye may be also." Imagine! Almighty God, Jehovah Jesus, wants us to live with Him forever. Not because of anything we have done but because of what He has done for us.

In 2 Corinthians 5:21 Paul states, "For He made Him to be sin for us, who knew no sin, that we might be made the righteousness of God in Him." In 2 Peter 2:24 Peter states, "Who His own self bare our sins in His body on the tree, that we, being dead to sins should live unto righteousness by whose stripes we are healed."

In Titus 3:5 Paul states, "Not by works of righteousness which we have done, but according to His mercy He saved us by the washing of regeneration and renewing of the Holy Ghost." Jesus paid a price that we could not pay. Paul states in Romans 6:23,

"For the wages of sin is death, but the gift of God is eternal life through Jesus Christ our Lord." There is no other way to escape eternal death but by Jesus. Jesus is God who became a man so that men could become like God.

In John 1:1 and verse 14 John states, "In the beginning was the Word, and the Word was with God, and the Word was God, and the Word was made flesh and dwelt among us (and we beheld His glory as of the only begotten of the Father) full of grace and truth." Jesus Himself said in John 14:6, "I am the Way the Truth and the Life, no man cometh to the Father but by Me." Would you like to be like God one day? The only way that will ever happen is that we receive God's sacrifice for our sins. The world would have us to believe that there are several ways to be saved, but the Bible does not teach that. The Bible tells us that there is only one way, God's way, through trust in the gospel of Jesus Christ. Everyone can be saved, but everyone will not be saved because they are so stubborn and hard-hearted that they will not humble themselves before God. God wants everyone to be saved and has opened a channel whereby we may be saved. Romans 10:13 states, "Whosoever shall call upon the name of the Lord shall be saved."

The second coming will be in two parts, "The Rapture of the Saints and when Jesus will place his feet upon the earth the second time. In the first part of the second coming, Jesus will not set His feet upon the earth but will call all the redeemed up to that point both dead and alive to meet Him in the clouds. In 1 Thessalonians 4:13–18 Paul states, "But I would not have you to be ignorant, brethren, concerning them which are asleep, that you sorrow not even as others which have no hope. For if we believe that Jesus Died and rose again, even them which also sleep in Jesus will God bring with Him. For this we say unto you, by the word of the Lord, that we which are alive and remain unto the coming of the Lord shall not prevent them which are asleep. For the Lord Himself shall descend from heaven with a shout, and with the voice of the archangel, and with the trump of God, and the dead in Christ shall rise first, then we which are alive and remain shall be caught up together with them in the clouds to meet the Lord in the air, and so shall we ever be with the Lord. Wherefore comfort one another with these words."

Paul states in 1 Corinthians 15:51–52, "Behold, I show you a mystery, we shall not all sleep, but we shall be changed, in a moment, in the twinkling of an eye at the last trump. For the trumpet will sound, and the dead shall be raised incorruptible, and we shall be changed." But when will this be? We know from Scripture that it will happen, but we are not given the exact time. That is hidden within the will and mind of Almighty God. But be sure, He is coming back. After Jesus's resurrection He walked the earth showing Himself alive for forty days. But soon He must ascend back into heaven so that the Holy Spirit could come.

In John 14:16–18 Jesus said, "I will pray the Father, and He shall give you another Comforter that He may abide with you forever. Even the Spirit of Truth; whom the world cannot receive because it seeth Him not, neither knoweth Him; But ye know Him for He dwelleth with you and shall be in you." Jesus also states in John 16:7–8, "Nevertheless I tell you the truth; it is expedient for you that I go away; for if I go not away the Comforter will not come unto you; but if I depart I will send Him unto you and when He is come He will reprove the world of sin, and of righteousness and of judgment; of sin, because they believe not on Me; of righteousness because I go to my Father, and ye see Me no more; of judgment because the prince of this world is judged. When the Spirit of Truth is come, He will guide you into all truth."

In Acts 1:9–11 Luke states, "And when He had spoken these things, while they beheld, He was taken up and a cloud received Him out of their sight. And while they looked steadfastly toward heaven as He went up, behold, two men stood by them in white apparel; which also said, Ye men of Galilee, why stand ye gazing up into heaven? This same Jesus which is taken up from you into heaven shall so come in like manner as ye have seen Him go into heaven."

The doctrine of the trinity is confusing to many people. We must understand that there is only one True and Living God who reveals Himself to us in three personalities, God the Father, God the Son, and God the Holy Spirit. When we get to heaven, we will not see three thrones, but only one, and one seated upon the throne of the universe, the Lord God Almighty. To teach that God is three separate beings is to teach that there is more than one perfect being. NO! There is and has always been only one True and Living God who came to earth in the person of Jesus Christ to shed His perfect blood for our sins. The price demanded for our sins is a perfect sacrifice. Since there has only been one perfect being that has ever existed, then Almighty God must be the sacrifice offered. Almighty God came to earth as a man to pay the ultimate price for our sins. No other price is acceptable. We are drawn to God the Son, Jesus, by God the Holy Spirit, that we might come to know the love of God the Father. Do you believe that there is more than one perfect being? Believe what you may, but the Bible says that there is and has always been one perfect being, Jehovah Jesus, God in the flesh. There never has or never will be again one like Him. There is only one God, and He is coming again soon. Even so, come quickly, Lord Jesus!

CHAPTER II
THE JUDGMENT SEAT OF CHRIST

The judgment seat of Christ is for redeemed people to give account for their lives after they were saved. In Romans 14:10 Paul states, "For we shall all stand before the judgment seat of Christ." Again, in 2 Corinthians 5:10 Paul states, "For we must appear before the judgment seat of Christ that everyone may receive the things done in his body according to that he hath done whether it be good or bad." At this judgment the redeemed are to give account for their life's works, not their sins. Jesus took care of the penalty for our sins in His death on the cross.

In Romans 8:1 Paul states, "There is therefore now no condemnation to them which are in Christ Jesus." Knowing that we must give account for our own selves we must not pass judgment on the sins of others. Jesus will judge all saved people. At this judgment we will either receive or lose rewards. This judgment has nothing to do with whether, or not one goes to heaven or hell. Again, Jesus took care of that in His death on the cross. His death was a substitutionary death. The wages of sin is death and Jesus took our place.

Paul tells us of the judgment seat of Christ in 1 Corinthians 3:11–15. "According to the grace of God, which is given me, as a wise master builder I have laid the foundation and another buildeth thereon. But let every man take heed how he buildeth thereupon. For other foundation can no man lay than that that is laid which is Jesus Christ. Now, if any man, build upon this foundation gold, silver, precious stones, wood, hay, stubble, every man's work shall be made manifest for the day shall declare it, because it shall be revealed by fire and the fire shall try every man's work of what sort it is. If any man's work abide which he has built thereupon he shall receive a reward. If any man's work be burned up, he shall suffer loss but himself shall be saved so as by fire."

Some people think that all they need to do is to be saved and then they can live their lives any way they please. The Bible does not teach that. Although we are eternally saved, we must still give account to God for the way we have lived our lives after we were saved. Those who have loved and served the Lord will be rewarded but those who have wasted their lives in selfishness and self-centeredness will lose their rewards, that is, if they had any to start with. But on the other hand, some will rejoice over their service and love for Jesus in this life. We are deciding right now which way we want it to be. Either way, we have no one to blame but ourselves because we will give account for ourselves and no one else.

That is why Paul asked in Romans 14:10-12, "Why do you judge your brother? Again, why do you regard you brother with contempt? For we shall all stand before the judgment seat of Christ. For it is written, "As I live, saith the Lord, every knee shall bow to Me, and every tongue shall give praise to God. So, then each one of us shall give account of himself to God." If we spent more time dealing with our own affairs, we would not have the time to judge our brethren. Everyone shall stand before Jesus to be judged.

In John 5:22–23 Jesus said, "For the Father judges no man but has given all judgment to the Son in order that all may honor the Son even as they honor the Father. He who does not honor the Son does not honor the Father who sent Him." Jesus is both our

Saviour and our Judge. God the Father deals with all creation through the Son. Jesus created everything and He sustains everything. The writer to the book of Hebrews records in Hebrews 1:1–3. "God who at sundry times and in divers manners spake in time past unto the fathers by the prophets hath in these last days spoken unto us by His Son, whom He hath appointed heir of all things, by whom He also made the worlds; who being the brightness of His glory and the express image of His person, and upholding all things by the word of His power, when He by Himself purged our sins, sat down on the right hand of the Majesty on high."

So, we conclude from Scripture that the judgment seat of Christ will be for all the redeemed both dead and alive up to this point of the rapture which is the first part of the second coming of Christ. Again, at this time Jesus does not set His feet upon the earth but will call all the redeemed to meet Him in the clouds. That will be a time of chaos such as this world has never seen. Airplanes without pilots, ships without captains, cars without drivers, cradles without babies. A world in total chaos. Of course, the world leaders left at that time will come up with some reason for the terrible happening. I do not know what it will be, but it is the perfect time for the Antichrist to step in and take over control.

We must remember that at the rapture of the saints the world will still go on. It will plunge into the most terrible time ever known to man. The great tribulation period which we will discuss later. If you want to escape that madness you need to receive Jesus as your Saviour now. All that you must do is confess your sins to God and trust His gospel. God's salvation is a free, gift to you if you will just reach out and take it. We are saved by grace through faith. Will you place your faith in Jesus right now?

CHAPTER III
THE TRIBULATION PERIOD [7 YEARS]

At the rapture of the saints not everyone will be caught up in the clouds because at that time everyone on earth will not be redeemed by the blood of God's Lamb, Jesus. Not everyone will believe the gospel. While the redeemed are caught up, the world below goes on. They will move into the most terrible time this world has ever known for a period of seven years. It is called the Great Tribulation. If you do not want to live in that period, you need to believe the gospel and receive Jesus as your Saviour NOW! There will be catastrophes such as this world has never seen before and will never see again. The tribulation period will serve two main purposes. It will be a time when God will vent His anger on a Christ rejecting world, and God is preparing Israel to finally receive Jesus as their promised Messiah.

In Matthew 24:21 Jesus said, "For then shall there be great tribulation such as was not since the beginning of the world to this time, no, nor ever shall be." There will be earthquakes, storms, volcano eruptions, sickness, disease of every sort, raging fires, drought, lack of water and food, darkness in the middle of the day, etc.

In Jeremiah 30:7 Jeremiah states, "Alas! For that day is great so that none is like it; it is even the time of Jacob's trouble."

In Revelation 6:12–17 John states, "And I beheld when the angel had opened the sixth seal, and lo, there was a great earthquake, and the sun became black as sackcloth of hair, and the moon became as blood, and the stars of heaven fell unto the earth, even as a fig tree casteth her untimely figs when she is shaken of a mighty wind, and the heavens departed as a scroll when it is rolled together, and every mountain and island were moved out of their places and the kings of the earth, and the great men, and the rich men, and the chief captains, and the mighty men, and every bondman, and every free man hid themselves in the dens and in the rocks of the mountains. And said to the rocks and mountains, fall on us, and hide us from the face of Him that sitteth on the throne, and from the wrath of the Lamb, for the great day of His wrath is cone, and who shall be able to stand?" Never has there been such misery, pain, and tribulation such as will be during that seven years on earth. At that time hell will be turned lose on earth. We must remember that although most of the remaining people will be wicked and ungodly there are still a few people left who will see the light, and there will be children born during that period. If that was not so, then who would be left to enter the Millennium Kingdom after the tribulation period? We will discover in our later study that Jesus is coming back to rescue those people or Satan would destroy them all. At the end of this period there will be a mighty battle between the forces of good and the forces of evil. Just when it appears that evil will prevail, Jesus will make His appearance on earth the second time. I pray that you will think about these terrible events and turn to Jesus for salvation now. There is no other way to escape.

In Hebrews 2:3 the writer of the Hebrews asked, "How shall we escape if we neglect so great salvation?"

In Romans 10:9 Paul tells us, "If thou shalt confess with thy mouth the Lord, Jesus, and believe in thine heart that God hath raised Him from the dead, thou shalt be saved."

In Acts 4:12 Luke records, "Neither is there salvation in any other for there is none other name under heaven given among men whereby we must be saved."

In John 14:6 Jesus said, "I am the Way, the Truth, and the Life; no man cometh to the Father but by Me." That will be a terrible time on earth. But there is a way to escape. Believing in the gospel message is the only escape. If you believe that Jesus, the Son of God, died on the cross at mount Calvary, was buried, and rose from the dead, God promised that He would save you. We have the word of God concerning that matter and God cannot lie. Do you believe the word of God?

CHAPTER IV
THE SECOND COMING OF CHRIST

In the second part of the second coming of Christ He is coming back to earth. In Revelation 19:11–21 John states, "And I saw heaven opened, and behold a white horse; and He that sat upon him was called Faithful and True, and in righteousness He doth judge and make war. His eyes were as a flame of fire, and on His head were many crowns; and He had a name written that no man knew but He Himself. And He was clothed with a vesture dipped in blood, and His name is called the Word of God. And the armies which were in heaven followed Him upon white horses, clothed in fine linen, white and clean. And out of His mouth goeth a sharp sword that with it He should smite the nations; and He shall rule them with a rod of iron, and He treadeth the wine press of the fierceness and wrath of Almighty God. And He had on His vesture and on His thigh a name written, King of Kings and Lord of Lords." Jesus promised on more than one occasion that He is coming back to set things right.

He said in John 14:2,3, "I go to prepare a place for you, and if I go and prepare a place for you, I will come again and receive you unto Myself that where I am there ye may be also." When Jesus makes His second entry into this world it will be far different than the first time. He came the first time as a lowly, humble, baby, grew up to be thirty-three years old, died on a cross, was buried, and rose from the dead on the third day, and now is ascended back into heaven. But this time He is coming back as a conquering King taking vengeance on His enemies.

In Jude verses 14 and 15, Jude proclaims, "And Enoch also, the seventh from Adam prophesied of these things saying, "Behold, the Lord cometh with ten, thousands of His saints, to execute judgment upon all, and to convince all that are ungodly among them of all their ungodly deeds which they have ungodly committed, and of all their hard speeches which ungodly sinners have spoken against Him." Zechariah states in Zechariah 14:12. "And this shall be the plague when the Lord will smite all people that have fought against Jerusalem; their flesh shall consume away while they stand upon their feet, and their eyes shall consume away in their holes. And their tongue shall consume away in their mouth." Paul again states in 2 Thessalonians 1:7–10, "And to you who are troubled rest with us, when the Lord Jesus shall be revealed from heaven with His mighty angels, in flaming fire taking vengeance on them that know not God, and that obey not the gospel of our Lord Jesus Christ, who shall be punished with everlasting destruction from the presence of the Lord and from the glory of His power when He shall come to be glorified in His saints and admired in all them that believe." One day God is going to have His revenge on a world that rejected His love. It will indeed be the great and terrible day of the Lord. Men and Satan will have no power to stand against the power of Almighty God. God has warned, and warned, and warned that that day is coming when the mighty of this world will see what awesome power God has. Praise God! Jesus is coming again!

A-The Battle of Armageddon

The Battle of Armageddon is also referred to as, "The Great and Terrible Day of the Lord." It will occur immediately after the tribulation period. Jesus will return with the armies of heaven and all the raptured saints up to that time. Some believe that the armies of heaven and the raptured saints will fight the battle with Jesus. According to Scripture Jesus will fight this battle by Himself. It is His time of revenge on a Christ rejecting world. Jesus does not need an army to help Him. He is Almighty God. He can swat Satan, the Antichrist, the False Prophet and all their armies like one swatting a fly. He will fight with the sword of His mouth which is the Word of God. All He must do is to speak it and it is done. At that time the whole universe will see His power.

Zephaniah 1:14–18 states, "The great day of the Lord is near, it is near, and hasteth greatly, even the voice of the day of the Lord; the mighty man shall cry bitterly. The day is a day of wrath, a day of trouble and distress, a day of wasteness and desolation, a day of darkness and gloominess, a day of clouds and thick darkness, a day of the trumpet and alarm against the fenced cities, and against the high towers. And I will bring distress upon men that they shall walk like blind men, because they have sinned against the Lord; and their blood shall be poured out as dust, and their flesh as the dung. Neither their silver nor gold will be able to deliver them in the day of the Lord's wrath; but the whole land shall be devoured by the fires of His jealousy; for He shall make even a speedy riddance of them that dwell in the land."

Revelation 1:16 states, "And He had in His right hand seven stars; and out of His mouth went a sharp two-edged sword."

Revelation 19:2 states, "For true and righteous are His judgments; for He hath judged the great whore which did corrupt the earth with her fornication, and hath avenged the blood of His servants at her hand."

Revelation 19:15 states, "And out of His mouth goeth a sharp sword that with it He should smite the nations, and He shall rule them with a rod of iron; and He treadeth the winepress of the fierceness and wrath of Almighty God. And He had on His vesture and on His thigh a name written, King of Kings and Lord of

Lords." Jesus is coming back the second time to fight with the fury of Almighty God. Nothing will be able to stand before Him. It will be a great day for the redeemed of God.

Revelation 16:16 states, "And He gathered them together into a place called in the Hebrew tongue Armageddon."

Zechariah 14:1–6 states. "Behold, the day of the Lord cometh and thy spoil shall be divided in the midst of thee. For I will gather all nations against Jerusalem to battle, and the city shall be taken, and the houses rifled, and the women ravished, and half of the city shall go forth into captivity, and the residue of the people shall not cut off the city. Then shall the Lord go forth and fight against those nations, as when He fought in the day of battle. And His feet shall stand that day upon the Mount of Olives, which is before Jerusalem on the east side and the Mount of Olives shall cleave in the midst thereof toward the east and toward the west, and there shall be a very great valley, and half the mountain shall remove toward the north and half of it toward the south and ye shall flee to the valley of the mountains. And ye shall flee like as ye fled from before the earthquake in the days of Uzziah of Judah, and the Lord thy God shall come and all the saints with Him. And it shall come to pass in that day that the light shall not be clear, nor dark, but it shall be one day which shall be known to the Lord, not day, nor night, but it shall come to pass that at evening time it shall be light."

The prophet Joel states in Joel 2:30–32, And I will show wonders in the heavens and in the earth, blood, fire, and pillars of smoke. The sun shall turn to darkness and the moon into blood before the great and terrible day of the Lord. And it shall come to pass that whosoever shall call upon the name of the Lord shall be deliverance. For in Mount Zion and in Jerusalem shall be delivered as the Lord hath said, and in the remnant whom the Lord shall call."

B-The Antichrist and the False Prophet

Satan has always wanted to be God. We know that can never happen because there is only one precious God. Because Satan can never be God, he does all he can to copy God. Because of that there is a Holy Trinity and an unholy trinity. The Holy Trinity is made up of God the Father, God the Son, and God the Holy Spirit. The unholy trinity is made up of Satan (the great dragon), the Antichrist, (the beast), and the false prophet. The Antichrist and the false prophet carry out the will of Satan.

Revelation 19:20 and 21 states, "And the beast was taken and with him the false prophet that wrought miracles before him with which he deceived them that had received the mark of the beast, and them that worshipped his image. These both were cast alive into a lake of fire burning with brimstone. And the remnant were slain with the sword of Him that sat upon the horse, which sword proceeded out of His mouth; and all the fowls were filled with their flesh." At the end of the tribulation period when Jesus returns to earth the second time the forces of good and evil will meet in battle. The false prophet carries out the will of the beast who carries out the will of Satan. John portrays the antichrist and the false prophet as two beasts, one rising up out of the sea and one rising up out of the earth. The antichrist will perform a false resurrection copying Jesus.

In Revelation 13:1–4 John states, "And I stood upon the sand of the sea and saw a beast rise up out of the sea having seven heads and ten horns and upon his head ten crowns and upon his heads the name of blasphemy. And the beast which I saw was like unto a leopard, and his feet were as the feet of a bear and his mouth as the mouth of a lion and the dragon (Satan) gave him his power, and his seat of great authority. And I saw one of his heads as it were wounded to death and his deadly wound was healed and all the world wondered after the beast. And they worshipped the dragon which gave power unto the beast, and they worshipped the beast, saying, who is like unto the beast? Who is able to make war with him?" The antichrist will pull off a false resurrection that will deceive the whole world and they will follow after him and worship him.

Jesus warned of this in John 5:43 when He stated, "I come in My Father's name and ye receive Me not; if another shall come in his own name him ye will receive." For some people it is easier to believe a lie than it is the truth. The devil is a liar and the whole world will follow him.

Then in Revelation 13:11–14 John states, "And I beheld another beast coming up out of the earth. And he exerciseth all the power of the first beast before him and caused the earth and them that dwell therein to worship the first beast whose deadly wound was healed. And doth great wonders so that he maketh fire come down from heaven on the earth in the sight of men. And deceiveth them that dwell on the earth by means of those miracles which he had the power to do in the sight of the beast saying to them that dwell on the earth that they should make an image to the beast which had the wound by a sword and did live." The unholy trinity is at work deceiving as many innocent souls as possible and condemning them to an eternal torment in hell. When Jesus returns to earth the second time, He will put an end to that horrible trinity. The great battle of Armageddon is about to be fought.

In Revelation 19:19–21 John tells us, "And I saw the beast and the kings of the earth, and their armies gathered to make war against Him that sat on the horse and against his army. And the beast was taken and with him the false prophet that wrought miracles before him which he deceived them that had received the mark of the beast and them that worshipped the image. These were both cast alive into a lake of fire burning with brimstone. And the remnant was slain with the Sword of Him that sat upon the horse which sword proceedeth out of His mouth, and all the fowl were filled with their flesh." This event is also referred to as, The Great Supper of the Lord.

In Revelation 19:17 John states, "And I saw an angel standing in the sun and he cried with a loud voice saying to all the fowls that fly in the midst of the heaven, "Come and gather yourselves together unto the supper of the great God." So many people will die that it will take seven months to cleanse the land for the coming Millennium Kingdom.

Ezekiel 39:12 states, "And seven months shall the house of Israel bury them that they may cleanse the land." We cannot imagine how foul-smelling and nasty it will be from all those rotten bodies of men and horses. But the land will be cleansed, and the Millennium Kingdom will begin after the judgment of the nations at the end of the battle. It is at this point that Satan will be incarcerated for a thousand years.

C-Satan is bound for a thousand years in the bottomless pit

Revelation 20:1–3 records, "And I saw an angel come down from heaven having the key to the bottomless pit and a great chain in his hand. And he laid hold on the dragon, that old serpent, which is called the devil and Satan, and bound him a thousand years and cast him into the bottomless pit and shut him up and set a seal upon him that he should not deceive the nations any more till the thousand years should be fulfilled; and after that he must be loosed a little season." After the battle of Armageddon an angel will descend from heaven with the key to a bottomless pit and a great chain, unbreakable to bind Satan. He will be in the abyss during the thousand years millennium reign of Christ upon earth. There are already some angels in the abyss because we find that during the tribulation period, they will be loosed under the sounding of the fifth and sixth trumpet judgments. These are some of the angels that fought with Satan when he first tried to overthrow God and take over heaven. Lucifer wants to be God.

Isaiah 14:12–14 states, "How art thou fallen from heaven o Lucifer, son of the morning! How art thou cut down to the ground which didst weaken the nations! For thou hast said in thine heart, I will ascend into heaven, I will exalt my throne above the stars of God, I will sit also upon the mount of the congregation in the sides of the north; I will ascend above the heights of the clouds; I will be like the Most High." At one time Lucifer was a high-ranking angel in God's order of angels until iniquity was found in him, Ezekiel 28:17–19 speaks of the fall of Lucifer. "Thine heart was lifted up because of thy beauty, thou hast corrupted thy wisdom by reason of thy brightness; I will cast thee to the ground, I will lay thee before kings that they may behold thee. Thou hast defiled thy sanctuaries by the multitude of thine iniquities; therefore, will I bring forth a fire from the midst of thee, it shall devour thee, and I will bring thee to ashes upon the earth in the sight of them that behold thee. All that know thee among the people shall be astonished at thee; thou shalt be a terror and never shalt thou be anymore."

Satan's doom has already been decreed by God and it will come to pass in its time. Lucifer was a high-ranking angel in heaven but somehow iniquity was found in him. How it got into heaven, I guess we will not know until the end when we will know and understand all things. Sin is powerful. It took control of a high, ranking angel who was in the very presence of God. Sin is so powerful that you and I have no chance against it without the help of God. No power is greater than God and one day all creation will get what is rightfully coming to them. Not only did Lucifer fall from heaven he also took with him many other angels that fell for his lies. God will not tolerate sin under any circumstance, and we need to learn that lesson from the people and events found in the word of God.

In 2 Peter 2:4 Peter gives us an example of how serious God is about sin. "God spared not the angels that sinned but cast them down to hell and delivered them into chains of darkness to be reserved unto judgment." God will let no one by with sin. All sin will be paid for one way or another. We know that all the fallen angels that were cast down are not all confined to hell right now. They are the demons that Satan uses to carry out his ungodly work in this world. Demons are fallen angels. Satan's heavenly army was probably like any other army having soldiers with different ranks. Those who are now in chains in the abyss and those that are in hell were probably part of the leadership of Satan's army. The ordinary fallen angels were probably equal to a private in our earthly army and are still loosed in the atmosphere who are the demons that now carry out Satan's will. Hell was not originally prepared for the souls of men but for Lucifer and the fallen angels. But if people rebel against God, they too will one day enter the eternal lake of fire to suffer in agony for ever and ever.

In Matthew 25:41 Jesus said, "Then shall He say unto them on the left hand, depart from Me, ye cursed into everlasting fire prepared for the devil and his angels." In Revelation 14:9–11 John records, "And the third angel followed them saying with a loud voice, if any man worship the beast and his image, and receive his mark in his forehead or in his hand, the same shall drink of the wine of the wrath of God, which is poured out without mixture into the cup of His indignation, and he shall be tormented with fire and brimstone in the presence of the holy angels and in the presence of the Lamb. And the smoke of their torment ascendeth up for ever and ever and they have no rest day or night who worship the beast and his image, and whosoever receiveth the mark of his name." God is love and does not want to see anyone suffer in the lake of fire for eternity no matter what age they may live in. The eternal torment is beyond our imagination.

In Luke chapter 16 we find the account of Lazarus and the rich man. The rich man died and went to hell. Lazarus died and went to Abraham's bosom. Verse 24 states of the rich man who went to hell, "And in hell he lifted up his eyes, being in torment, and seeth Abraham afar off and Lazarus in his bosom. And he cried out and said, "Father Abraham, have mercy on me and send Lazarus that he may dip the tip of his finger in water and cool my tongue for I am tormented in this flame." But it was to no avail. Hell is real! God does not want to see anyone go to that place of eternal torment. But if people reject His love shown in the person of Jesus Christ that is exactly where they will go. God spared none of the angels that rebelled against Him, and He will spare no person who rebels against Him now. God extends His love to everyone, but we must freely receive His love.

2 Peter 3:9 states, "The Lord is not slack concerning His promise as some men count slackness, but is longsuffering to usward not willing that any should perish but that all should come to repentance." God is in the saving business and has now done all that He can do to redeem human souls. But it must be done His way. The Bible is very plain in showing that salvation is either His way or no way. The other alternative is eternity in hell. The choice is yours.

D-The Judgment of the Nations.

The judgment of the nations is also referred to as "The Sheep and Goat Judgment." In Matthew 25:31–34, 41, 46 Jesus said, "When the Son of Man shall come in His glory and all the holy angels with Him, then shall He sit upon the throne of His glory; and before Him shall be gathered all nations; and He shall separate the one from the other as a shepherd divideth his sheep from his goats. And He shall set the sheep on His right hand and the goats on the left. Then shall the King say unto them on His right hand, come ye blessed of My Father; enter the kingdom prepared for you from the foundation of the world. Then shall He say unto them on the left, depart from Me ye cursed into everlasting fire prepared for the devil and his angels. And these shall go away into everlasting punishment but the righteous to life eternal." After the battle of Armageddon there must be a judgment before the Millennium Kingdom period. Although millions will die during that battle everyone will not be killed. The survivors will be both good and bad. There must be a separation between the righteous and the unrighteous. The righteous will enter the Millennium Kingdom and the unrighteous will enter hell or eternal punishment for rebellion against God.

In Joel 3:11, 12 Joel states, "Assemble yourselves and come all ye heathen and gather yourselves together round about; thither cause thy mighty ones to come down o Lord. Let the heathen be wakened and come up to the valley of Jehoshaphat, for there I will sit to judge the heathen round about." This judgment will come when the Son of Man comes in His glory at the end of the tribulation period. Those who were taken up into the clouds at the rapture of the saints and those righteous which died during the tribulation period will reign with Christ during the Millennium Kingdom.

In Revelation 20:4 John states, "And I saw thrones and they that sat upon them and judgment was given unto them, and I saw the souls of them that were beheaded for the witness of Jesus and for the word of God and which had not worshipped the beast neither his image, neither had received his mark upon their foreheads or in their hands, and they lived and reigned with Christ a thousand years. Blessed and holy is he that hath part in the first resurrection on such the second death hath no power, but they shall be priests of God and shall reign with Him a thousand years."

Many will come through the tribulation period. Who do you think Jesus is coming back for? There must be someone to enter the Millennium Kingdom or else who will Christ rule and reign over? Jesus will sit upon the throne of David as King of Kings and Lord of Lords. He will have a government on earth during the Millennium Kingdom. Of course, Jesus does not need the redeemed to help Him rule His kingdom, but that is part of the reward promised to all who have trusted and served Him while on earth. There will be various degrees of ruling and that will be determined by Jesus who is King and absolute Monarch. In the parable of the talents different amounts were distributed to the servants and each was expected to serve according to what they had been given. What are you doing with what Jesus has given you? One day soon it will be far more important than what you now think.

That is why David said in Psalm 100:2 "Serve the Lord with gladness." Our position will be determined by what we do now when our Lord returns to judge the nations and set up His Millennium Kingdom. It is at that point that our position in the kingdom will be given. Therefore, every day is an important day in our service for Jesus.

E-The Marriage of the Lamb

Of all the end time events this is the most difficult to identify and to put in its proper place. We know that the bridegroom is Jesus. In Matthew chapter nine the disciples of John the Baptist were questioning Jesus about fasting and Jesus referred to Himself as the Bridegroom. Matthew 9:14–15 states, "Then came to Him the disciples of John, saying, why do we and the Pharisees fast oft, but thy disciples fast not?" And Jesus said unto them, "Can the children of the bridegroom mourn as long as the bridegroom is with them?" But the days will come when the bridegroom shall be taken from them and then shall they fast." Jesus was referring to His ascension back into heaven. Jesus is the bridegroom but who is the bride? There are several explanations as to who the bride is. We must remember that we are dealing with several groups of people but one day they will all be brought together as one. The Old Testament saints, the New Testament saints, the tribulation saints and the Millennium saints. We must also remember that God is no respecter of persons. He does not think more of one generation of people than another nor does He show respect to any age in time. Do you think that some people are going to be left out of the bride just because they existed in the wrong period of time?

In the New Testament Paul identifies the bride as the New Testament church, but does he mean only the New Testament church? Are some of the redeemed going to be left out just because they were born in the wrong period in time? I do not think so. It is hard to pin down exactly when the marriage of the Lamb will take place. Some believe that the marriage will take place at the rapture of the saints when all the redeemed up to that point go to meet the Lord in the clouds. But what about the tribulation saints and the Millennium saints? Are they going to be left out of the bride? I do not think so. The Hebrew weddings took place in several different stages.

Dr. John Mac Arthur states in his study Bible, "Hebrew weddings consisted of several phases; 1) betrothal (often when the couple were children); 2) presentation (the festivities often lasting several days that proceeded the ceremony); 3) the ceremony (the exchanging of vows). The church was betrothed to Christ by His sovereign choice in eternity past, and will be presented to Him at the rapture of the saints. The final supper will signify the end of the ceremony. The symbolic meal will take place at the establishment of the Millennium Kingdom and last throughout the 1,000-year period. While the term "bride" often refers to the church it ultimately expands to include all the redeemed of all ages."1

Finis Dake in his study Bible states, "The word bride is used only five times in connection with believers. The word, "bridegroom" is used ten times in connection with believers. All those passages refer to believers who will live in the New Jerusalem, which is the bride, the Lamb's wife."2 All the redeemed will make up the bride no matter what age they existed in. No redeemed individual will be left out of the bride. One day all the redeemed of God will live with Him in the city of New Jerusalem.

Revelation 21:9–14, 24 states, "And there came unto me one of the seven angels which had the seven vials full of the seven last plagues, and talked with me, saying, come hither, I will show thee the bride, the Lamb's wife. And he carried me away in the spirit to a great and high mountain, and showed me that great city, the holy Jerusalem, descending out of heaven from God. Having the glory of God; and her light was like unto a stone most precious, even like a jasper stone, clear as crystal; and had a wall great and high, and had twelve gates, and at the gates twelve angels, and names written thereon which are the names of the twelve tribes of the children of Israel; on the east three gates, on the north three gates, on the south three gates, and on the west three gates. And the wall of the city had twelve foundations, and in them the names of the of the twelve apostles of the Lamb. And the nations of them which are saved shall walk in the light of it." All redeemed people will be part of the bride. Have you been redeemed by the blood of the Lamb?

CHAPTER V

THE MILLENNIUM REIGN

The term "millennium" means, "one thousand." It has been promised in both the old and new testaments that there would be a time in which Jesus would rule on earth for a thousand years. This is the kingdom that Israel has so long looked for. Revelation 20:1–3 states, "And I saw an angel come down from heaven having the key to the bottomless pit, and a great chain in his hand. And he laid hold on the dragon, the old serpent, which is the devil, and Satan, and bound him a thousand years. And cast him into the bottomless pit, and shut him up, and set a seal upon him that he should deceive the nations no more till the thousand years should be fulfilled. After that he must be loosed a little season."

The Millennium Kingdom will be after the battle of Armageddon. We cannot imagine how it will be to live in a world without the devil. It will be as it was meant to be in the Garden of Eden before man fell. There will be peace on earth and good will toward all people. Even the characters of nature will be affected. Isaiah 11:4–9 states, "With righteousness shall He judge the poor and reprove with equity for the meek of the earth, and He shall smite the earth with the rod of His mouth, and with the breath of His lips shall He slay the wicked. And righteousness shall be the girdle of His loins, and faithfulness the girdle of His reins. The wolf also shall dwell with the lamb, and the calf and young lion and the fatling together, and a little child shall lead them, and the cow and the bear shall feed together; their young ones shall lie down together, and the lion shall eat straw like the ox. And the suckling child shall play on the hole of the asp, and the weaned child shall put his hand on the cockatrice's den. They shall not hurt nor destroy in all My holy mountain; for the earth shall be full of the knowledge of the Lord as the waters cover the earth." This will be a time such as this world has never known since the fall of Adam. The whole world will be at peace. Satan will be bound during the Millennium Kingdom. All the raptured and tribulation saints will be together with Jesus with more love than we have ever felt before. God is love and pure love will be present with us. God promised and it is impossible for God to lie because every word that proceeds out of His mouth is truth. The redeemed are heirs of all that God has.

In Romans 8:16–17 Paul tells us, "The Spirit itself beareth witness with our spirit that we are the children of God. And if children, then heirs of God and joint heirs with Christ." All Saints will not have the same degree of rule in the kingdom. Our position will be determined by what we do for Christ here on earth. Some will have high places of rule while others will have lower places of rule, but all saints of God will rule with Christ in some area.

In Revelation 5:9–10 John states, "Thou hast made us unto our God kings and priests; and we shall reign on earth." The Millennium Kingdom is the period between the resurrection of the righteous and the resurrection of the wicked. Jesus refers to those two judgments in John 5:28–29. "Marvel not at this, for the hour is coming in which all that are in the graves shall hear His voice and shall come forth, they that have done good unto the resurrection of life, and they that have done evil unto the resurrection of damnation." The Millennium Kingdom will have a theocratic form of government in which Christ is Supreme Ruler over everyone. He will be the Supreme Dictator. But He will be a good Dictator.

In Daniel 7:13–14 Daniel informs us, "I saw in the night visions, and behold, one like the Son of Man came with the clouds of heaven and came to the Ancient of Days and they brought Him near before me. And there was given Him dominion, and glory, and a kingdom, that all people, nations, and languages should serve Him; His dominion is an everlasting dominion which shall not pass away, and His kingdom that which shall not be destroyed." His seat of government shall be rebuilt Jerusalem. It will be the capitol of the world and the central place of worship.

Isaiah 2:1–4 states, "The word that Isaiah the son of Amoz saw concerning Judah and Jerusalem. And it shall come to pass in the last days that the mountain of the Lord's house shall be established in the top of the mountains and shall be exalted above the hills and all nations shall flow into it. And many people will go and say, "Come ye, and let us go up to the mountain of the Lord, to the house of the God of Jacob, and He will teach us His ways and we will walk in His paths out of Zion shall go forth the law and the word of the Lord from Jerusalem. And He shall judge among the nations and shall rebuke many people, and they shall beat their swords into plowshares and their spears into pruninghooks. Nation shall not lift up sword against nation neither shall they learn war anymore."

We must remember that just because people adhere to God's laws and even attempt to worship does not mean that their heart is right with God. As long as they are in human flesh there will be the presence of self-will. Some people will still have a rebellious heart. Just as today some people live a lie, so shall it be in that day. They are living according to the laws of that time, but their heart is not in it. As long as there is flesh present there will be fleshly lusts and desires. If that was not so what would be the use in having laws. Although Christ is present, so is the flesh. Because man has a rebellious heart Satan will find it very easy to put together another army to go against God one last time when he is released from the abyss for a little time. Just like today some people just go through the motions of religion. Many unsaved people will pass through the Millennium Kingdom.

We must remember that over a period of a thousand years there will be many children born who have never known the temptations of Satan. They will be easy prey for Satan's lies. No matter what the age in time the wages of sin is death. If Satan could lie to the angels in heaven and get them to follow him, he will have no trouble with weak human beings. The temptation will be no different than it was in the Garden of Eden to begin with. God knows what is really in the human heart. In Jeremiah 17:10 God said, "I the Lord search the heart, I try the reins, even to give every man according to his ways, and according to the fruit of his doing."

In Revelation 2:23 Jesus states, "I am He which searcheth the reins and hearts; and I will give unto every one of you according to your works." Nothing is hidden from God no matter what period in history it may be. God is still all seeing and all knowing. Hebrews 4:13 records, "Neither is there any creature that is not manifest in His sight; but all things are naked and opened unto the eyes of Him with whom we have to do." The Millennium Kingdom will be glorious beyond our imagination. Paul tells us in 1 Corinthians 2:9, "As it is written, eye hath not seen, nor ear heard, neither has entered into the heart of man the things which God hath prepared for them that love Him." The question is, "Do you love Him!"

CHAPTER VI
SATAN IS LOOSED FOR A LITTLE SEASON

At the end of the thousand years, the word of God tells us that Satan will be released from the bottomless pit for a season. When he arrives, he will find it easy to deceive some of the people who have come out of the Millennium Kingdom. Revelation 20:7–9 states, "When the thousand years are expired Satan shall be loosed out of his prison and shall go out to deceive the nations which are in the four quarters of the earth, Gog and Magog to gather them together to battle, the number of whom is as the sand of the sea. And they went upon the breath of the earth and compassed the camp of the saints about and the beloved city and fire came down from God out of heaven and devoured them. And the devil that deceived them was cast into the lake of fire and brimstone where the beast and the false prophet are and shall be tormented day and night for ever and ever."

During the thousand years natural man has had ample opportunity to receive Jesus as their Saviour, and Lord. But some people are so rebellious and hardhearted that they will not yield to God's loving call and admit that they are lost, hell bound sinners. Our human nature is naturally depraved and wicked. Somehow, once again, Satan will deceive them into believing that they can overthrow Jesus who sits upon the throne in Jerusalem as King of Kings. Man has always had a problem with the "God syndrome."

Man wants to be God and Satan will deceive them into thinking they can, just like he did in the Garden of Eden in the beginning. That is exactly the reason Lucifer fell from heaven in the beginning. He wanted to overthrow Almighty God and reign as God. In his final effort he is still trying to do so. He will make his final march on Jerusalem where Christ sits on the throne.

In Isaiah 14:12–15 Isaiah speaks of the fall of Lucifer. "How art thou fallen from heaven o Lucifer, son of the morning! How art thou cut down to the ground which did weaken the nations! For thou hast said in thine heart, I will ascend into heaven, I will exalt my throne above the stars of God, I will set upon the mount of the congregation in the sides of the north. I will ascend above the heights of the clouds, I will be like the Most High. Yet thou shalt be brought down to hell, to the sides of the pit." The devil knows that his time is short. There is no hope for him, so he wants to drag as many human souls as possible to hell with him through trickery and deception. Satan is still deceiving people today. Isaiah tells us that hell is enlarging its borders every day with unbelieving souls who believe the lies of Satan. The devil is a liar and that is all he ever can be. Believe the word of God and do not trust in what other people say.

In John 8:44–45 Jesus is speaking to those who are the children of the devil. "Ye are of your father the devil and the lusts of your father ye will do. He was a murderer from the beginning and abode not in the truth because there is no truth in him. When he speaks a lie, he speaks of his own, for he is a liar and the father of it." The devil is a liar and has a world full of liars. Anything that goes contrary to the teachings of the Bible is a lie. The devils' greatest battle is to try to stomp out the word of God because it is absolute truth. If anyone tells us something they must be able to back it up with the word of God. This world is full of old wife's tales handed down through the ages and many people are falling for them. God does not just tell the truth. He is the truth.

As soon as Satan is loosed from his thousand years prison, he will start lying again. That is all he can ever do because that is what he is, a liar. Satan cannot hurt a child of God, but he can make us hurt ourselves by believing his lies. That is why we must live close to Jesus and study His word so that we do not fall into Satan's traps. He is the great deceiver, and we are no match with his wits unless we have the help of God's Holy Spirit that lives within us. Please do not be one of those people who believe in Satan's lies. Trust in the gospel and you can be saved. God does not want anyone to suffer in the eternal lake of fire with Satan and his crowd. But everyone who rejects the gospel of Jesus Christ will go there. Hell was not originally created for the souls of men, but that is where all unbelievers will go if they reject the gospel message as God's means of eternal salvation. Jesus Himself taught more lessons and preached more messages on hell than any other character in the Bible. He warned and warned people over, and over again because He did not want to see anyone go to that awful place of eternal torment.

In Matthew 10:28 Jesus said, "Fear not them which kill the body, but are not able to kill the soul, but rather fear him which is able to destroy both soul and body in hell." When Satan is released from the bottomless, pit he will return to fight one last battle against God and His people. That will be the final battle of the ages. After that battle there will be no more war. Jesus will then judge all unbelievers of all times and cast them into the lake of fire to be tormented for ever and ever. If you end up in the eternal lake of fire you will have no one to blame but yourself. You have been warned and given the opportunity to make your choice. Will you heed the warning now because your life may soon be gone? After death there is no more opportunity to be saved. Do not sin your day of grace away. Take advantage of your opportunity now.

CHAPTER VII
THE FINAL BATTLE

When Satan is released from the bottomless pit, he will return to make one last attempt to overthrow God. He will return to fight against God and His people. This will result in the final battle of the ages. After this battle God will put an end to Satan, the fallen angels, all his followers, and sin. This battle is preparing for a new time such as man has never seen. Revelation 20:7–10 states, "And when the thousand years were expired Satan shall be released out of his prison and shall go out to deceive the nations which are in the four quarters of the earth, Gog and Magog to gather them together to battle, the number of whom is as the sands of the sea. And they went up in the breadth of the earth and compassed the camp of the saints about and the beloved city, and fire came down from God out of heaven and devoured them. And the devil that deceived them was cast into the lake of fire where the beast and the false prophet are and shall be tormented day and night forever and ever."

Many people believe that Satan came from hell. The truth is that Satan has never yet been to hell. They picture Satan as a little red man with a pitchfork, horns, and a long, pointed tail. Nothing could be farther from the truth. According to the Bible, Lucifer is a beautiful angel. That is why he can make sin and disobedience to God appear to be beautiful and fulfilling to the lusts of our flesh. Sin is not beautiful no matter how much Satan tries to cover it up. Sin will kill and some people will be destroyed forever because of sin. Satan will make his last attempt to overthrow God and God will set him on fire forever and the devil shall be no more. Praise God! It is wonderful to know that one day soon there will be no more devil, no more sin, no more heartache, no more sickness, no more death, and no more pain. Jesus promised that He was preparing a place where there is no more of those things and more. So, now we wait.

CHAPTER VIII
THE GREAT WHITE THRONE OF JUDGMENT

As we have previously mentioned, there will be two major judgments concerning the destiny of the human soul. The judgment seat of Christ and the great white throne of judgment. The judgment seat of Christ is for the redeemed. It is for the purpose of handing out rewards for service rendered on earth and has nothing to do with salvation. The great white throne of judgment is for those who are not redeemed by the blood of the Lamb. They willfully chose not to trust the gospel of our Lord Jesus Christ. The judgment for rejection of the gospel has already been passed and now the sentencing will be carried out. The sentence for rejecting the sacrifice of Jesus for our sins is eternal death in the torments of the lake of fire.

In John 5:28 Jesus spoke of the two major judgments. "Marvel not at this, for the hour is coming in which all that are in the grave shall hear His voice and shall come forth, they that have done good unto the resurrection of life, and they that have done evil unto the resurrection of damnation." There are several other judgments, but these are the two major judgments. Jesus spoke of them in terms of two resurrections. The great white throne of judgment will come immediately after the final battle and is the final judgment that will take place upon the souls of men.

Revelation 20:11–15 states, "And I saw a great white throne and Him that sat on it from whose face the earth and the heavens fled away and there was found no more place for them. And I saw the dead small and great stand before God; and the books were opened, and another book was opened which is the book of life, and the dead were judged out of those things which were written in the books according to their works. And the sea gave up the dead which were in it; and death and hell delivered up the dead which were in them; and they were judged every man according to their works. And death and hell were cast into the lake of fire and whosoever was not found written in the book of life was cast into the lake of fire." The Judge on the throne is God, Jehovah Jesus. The Bible tells us clearly that all judgment is given to the Son, Jesus, God in the flesh. Jesus created all things, He sustains all things, and He will judge all things.

John 5:22 states, "For the Father judgeth no man, but hath committed all judgment to the Son." Jesus is God veiled in flesh for no man could see God the Father unveiled and live. Do you believe that there is more than one perfect being? In Ephesians4:4–6 Paul states, "There is one body, and one Spirit, even as ye are called in one hope of your calling; one Lord, one faith, one baptism, one God and Father of all who is above all, and through all, and in you all." The Lord God Almighty is the only one who could be the perfect sacrifice for our sins. Nothing else will do. Once again God became a man so that men could become like God. Only the blood of God in the person of Jesus Christ can atone for our sins.

Hebrews 10:4–6 states, "For it is not possible that the blood of bulls and goats should take away sins, wherefore when He cometh into the world, He saith, Sacrifice and offerings thou wouldest not, but a body hast thou prepared Me. In burnt offerings and sacrifices for sin thou hast had no pleasure." Almighty God came down to earth to shed His precious, perfect blood to redeem our souls. Jesus' death was a substitutionary death. At the great white throne of judgment all people who have rejected the love of God in Christ Jesus will be cast into the lake of fire for ever and ever. Those who have received Jesus as the sacrifice for their sins have already been judged as far as their salvation goes.

For all of us who have trusted in the gospel message, Jesus bore the penalty of our sin judgment on the cross of Mount Calvary and was raised the third day, conquering death, and securing and insuring our eternal life. Because He lives, we shall also live eternally with Him. The books out of which the Christ rejectors will be judged are the sixty-six books of our Bible. When we are redeemed by the blood of God's Lamb our names are recorded in the Lamb's book of life. Anyone whose name is not found written in the book of life will be cast into the lake of fire to suffer for ever and ever. Only the blood of God in the person of Jesus Christ can atone for our sins.

Hebrews 10:4–7 states, "For it is impossible that the blood of bulls and goats should take away sins. In burnt offerings and sacrifices for sin thou hast had no pleasure. Then said I, lo, I come (in the volume of the book it is written of me) to do thy will o God." Hell is real! Jesus said so many times. It is hot, tormenting fire and brimstone that will never end. Once a person enters hell there is no hope that they will ever get out. How sad that millions of people will stand before God at the great white throne of judgment only to hear, "Depart from Me for I never knew you." Because of a rebellious, hard heart they would not yield to Jesus. Will you stand before God at the great white throne of judgment only to hear those sad words? Confess your sins, repent, and ask Jesus to save you now, and you will never hear those sad words.

CHAPTER IX

THE RENEWING OF CREATION

For hundreds of years people have been asking, "Where will heaven be?" "What will it be like?" They are baffled whenever they are told that heaven will be right here on earth where we are now, but in a different situation. In Revelation 21:1–6 John tells us, "And I saw a new heaven and a new earth; for the first heaven and the first earth were passed away and there was no more sea. And I, John, saw the holy city, New Jerusalem, coming down from God out of heaven as a bride adorned for her husband. And I heard a great voice out of heaven saying, Behold, the tabernacle of God is with men, and He will dwell with them, and they shall be His people, and God Himself shall be with them, and be their God. And God shall wipe away all tears from their eyes; and there shall be no more death, neither sorrow, nor crying, neither shall there be any more pain; for the former things are passed away. And He that sat upon the throne said, Behold, I make all things new. And He said unto me, write; for these words are true and faithful. And He said unto me, it is done. I am Alpha and Omega, the beginning and the end."

There are many questions that we may ask concerning this subject and time will not permit us to cover them all so we will deal with those that are most clear. When the Bible speaks of destroying the world or the old order, it does not mean that God will explode the planet. The term "world" is used in at least three major ways throughout the Bible. First, it speaks of this round sphere of dirt upon which we live. Second, it refers to a Satanic, ungodly, world system that now dominates the people of this world. Third, it refers to humanity.

In John 3:16 Jesus said," For God so loved the world that He gave His only begotten Son that whosoever believeth in Him should not perish but have everlasting life." When God destroyed the world by water in Noah's day, He did not explode the planet. He washed everything off the face of the earth except eight just souls, Noah and his family. Since the fall of man there has been much pain and misery, but God has been right here with us through it all. God's word tells us that there will be a newer, brighter day ahead when this world will be restored as it was originally meant to be before the fall of man in the Garden of Eden. But before that day comes there must be many changes. There will be a renewing or remaking of everything.

In 2 Peter 3:10-13 Peter tells us of the renovation. "But the day of the Lord will come as a thief in the night in which the heavens shall pass away with a great noise, and the elements shall melt with fervent heat, the earth also and the works therein shall be burned up. Seeing then that all these things be dissolved what manner of persons ought ye to be in all holy conversation and goodness?" God destroyed the earth the first time with water. The second time He will burn it clean with fire.

Isaiah 34:4 records, "And all the host of heaven shall be dissolved, and the heavens shall be rolled together as a scroll." One day soon when God's plan is complete He will burn this earth clean with fire, renew everything, and the Holy City, New Jerusalem will be let down out of heaven and here we shall dwell with God for ever and ever as it was meant to be in the beginning in the Garden of Eden. The only ones who will be part of this glorious existence will be those who have trusted in the blood of God's Lamb, Jesus. Who are you trusting with your future? Everything will be made new, even you!

CHAPTER X

THE FINAL CALL

God does not want to see anyone go to hell. He has now done everything He can do to save people from going to that awful place called hell. We are not predestinated, meaning that God created some people to go to heaven and some to go to hell. We are predestinated to the point that we will go to one of two places, heaven or hell. Besides those two places there is no other place for our eternal soul to go. God created us to have a choice. We ourselves choose whether we will go to heaven or hell. It is our choice and millions of people are making the wrong choice. The devil will do anything to keep people from making the right choice. God is in the saving business. He wants to see everyone saved but that will not happen because people are too stubborn and hardhearted to yield to His call. It takes four things to be saved, the word of God, the conviction of sin, the power of the Holy Spirit, and a receptive human heart. Some people just will not yield to the convicting power of the Holy Spirit when they hear God's word.

In Revelation 22:17 John records God's final call for people to come to Him before He closes out His love letter to humanity, the Bible. "And the Spirit and the bride say COME, and let him that heareth say COME, and let him that is athirst say COME, and whosoever will, let him take of the water of life freely." One day soon time as we know it will be no more. God has spent thousands of years working on a plan so that we could be with Him forever. God loves everyone and He does not want to see anyone suffer in the lake of fire forever. For thousands of years God has been calling people to come to Him for eternal salvation and still people close their hearts and minds to His call. Now there is nothing else that God can do. No matter what you have done in the past or what you are doing right now God wants you to come to Him just like you are. Jesus is the water of life and God is offering everyone a free drink of His eternal, living water. The sacrifice of Jesus on the cross is a gift from God.

In Romans 6:23 Paul states, "The wages of sin is death but the gift of God is eternal life through Jesus Christ our Lord." God loves us so much He has held back nothing in order to possess our eternal soul. He left His throne in glory and came down to this wicked world as a man so that He could die on a cross and shed His perfect, precious blood as the price demanded for our sin. There is now nothing more that God can do to save people. He has given everything for us. All He wants us to do is to stop and survey our helpless, hopeless situation and reason with Him about our problem.

In Isaiah 1:18 God said, "Come now and let us reason together, though your sins be as scarlet, they shall be white as snow; though they be red like crimson they shall become as wool." Now all that we must do is to admit to God that we are lost hell bound sinners, ask for God's forgiveness, and ask Him to save us for Jesus' sake and He will. The blood of Jesus Christ will cleanse us from all our sins and save our souls. Eternal salvation is now free for the asking.

Psalm 103:10–17 tells us, "He hath not dealt with us after our sins; nor rewarded us according to our iniquities. For as the heaven is high above the earth how great is His mercy toward them that fear Him. As far as the east is from the west, so far hath

He removed our transgressions from us. Like a father pitieth his children so the Lord pitieth them that fear Him. For He knoweth our frame; He remembereth that we are dust. As for man, his days are as grass; as a flower of the field, so flourisheth. For the wind passeth over it and it is gone, and the place thereof shall it be no more. But the mercy of the Lord is from everlasting to everlasting on them that fear Him and His righteousness to children's children." We do not deserve anything, but God wants to give us everything.

David asked in Psalm 8:4 What is a man that thou art mindful of him? Or the son of man that thou visiteth him? The love of God for us is so deep it is beyond our imagination. In order to reach us He sent prophets, apostles and finally He came Himself in the person of Jesus Christ and we killed Him. If we got what we rightfully deserved, we would all suffer in the lake of fire forever. If Satan had his way that is exactly what would happen. But God intervened on our behalf with His love, mercy, and grace, and gave us a way to escape the everlasting torment for our sins. Nothing else can be said or done concerning our salvation. Now it is totally up to each individual. Will you be with Jesus at the judgment seat of Christ concerning your rewards, or will you stand before Him at the great white throne of judgment because you rejected God's love in the person of Christ Jesus? We cannot work for, or earn salvation, nor are we worthy of salvation. We are sinful creatures upon whom God has shown mercy.

In Titus 3:5 Paul tells us, "Not by works of righteous which we have done but according to His mercy He saved us." In Ephesians 2:8,9 Paul states, "For by grace are ye saved through faith and that not of yourselves it is the gift of God. Not of works lest any man should boast." God ends His word with one last call to come to Him. In John chapter 6, there were a large, number of disciples that had been following Jesus. Many of them were following Him for what they thought they could get out of Him.

In verses 60-65 He had given them a hard saying that they could not understand. Verses 66–69 John tells us, "From that time many of His disciples went back and walked no more with Him. Then said Jesus unto the twelve, Will ye also go away? Then Simon Peter answered and said, Lord, to whom shall we go? Thou hast the words of eternal life. And we believe and are sure that thou art that Christ, the Son of the living God." Do you believe as Peter did? Will you hear Him when He calls?

CONCLUSION

As we stated, thousands of people throughout the ages have asked, "WHAT'S NEXT?" Although we did not cover every subject concerning the end times, we have covered enough to lay out by Scripture the remaining events of the ages. I hope and pray that I have touched on some things that will help someone better understand what God plans for the remaining ages are. God hides nothing from His people. He is out in the open with everything He plans to do in the future. I also hope that something has been said that will lead someone to the Saviour if you are not already saved. In Genesis 18:17 God told Abraham, "Shall I hide from Abraham that thing which I do?"

He also said in Genesis 22:6–8 when God had commanded Abraham to take his son Isaac to the land of Moriah, build an alter and sacrifice him there. The Bible states, "And Abraham took the wood of the burnt offering and laid it upon Isaac his son, and he took the fire in his hand, and a knife, and they went both of them together father and son. And Isaac spake unto Abraham his father and said, my father, and he said, here am I son. And he said, behold the fire and the wood, but where is the lamb for the sacrifice? And Abraham said, my son, God will provide Himself a Lamb for a burnt offering, so they both went together." God has provided Himself as the sacrifice for our sins.

Four thousand years later when the time was right God sent His only begotten Son to be the sacrifice.

In John 1:29 as John was baptizing in the river Jordan the Bible records, "The next day John seeth Jesus coming unto him and said, "Behold the Lamb of God which taketh away the sin of the world." Then Paul states in Galatians 4:4–5 "When the fullness of time was come, God sent forth His Son, made of a woman, made under the law, to redeem them that were under the law that we might receive the adoption of sons." Now God has provided everything necessary for us to have an eternal home in heaven. Now it is up to you. Do you believe God? If you want to know more about His plans for the future, then read His book; read His Bible. Everything that we need to know is in the book. One day when we stand before God we will be without excuse.

BIBLIOGRAPHY

1. John Mac Arthur Study Bible, copyright 1997, pg. 2019
2. Finis Dake Bible, copyright 2014, pg. 528